WHY YOUR VOTE MATTERS

GARY HAMRICK

HARVEST HOUSE PUBLISHERS
EUGENE, OREGON

Cover design by Kyler Dougherty

Cover images © Todd Trapani / Pexels; vitalik19111992, jakkapan21 / Getty Images

For bulk, special sales, or ministry purchases, please call 1-800-547-8979. Email: CustomerService@hhpbooks.com

This logo is a federally registered trademark of the Hawkins Children's LLC. Harvest House Publishers, Inc., is the exclusive licensee of this trademark.

Why Your Vote Matters
Copyright © 2024 by Gary Hamrick
Published by Harvest House Publishers
Eugene, Oregon 97408
www.harvesthousepublishers.com

ISBN 978-0-7369-9243-5 (pbk)
ISBN 978-0-7369-9244-2 (eBook)

Printed in the United States of America

24 25 26 27 28 29 30 31 32 / SK-BP / 10 9 8 7 6 5 4 3 2 1

WHY YOUR VOTE MATTERS

A Biblical Perspective
for the Soul of America

Since our country's earliest days, we have had the privilege of being able to vote. Through the political process, we have a voice in helping to choose which candidates and policies we believe are best for the good of our nation and are honoring to God. All through Scripture, we read repeatedly about how God used His people to speak truth to power and influence government. Today, the right to vote allows us the opportunity to do that as well. No aspect of society should be viewed as being beyond our faith's influence.

Historically, pastors have played a critical role in teaching how faith should shape our politics. During the decades before and after the Revolutionary War in colonial America, many pastors understood their duty to stand in the pulpit and use God's Word as the lens through which they were to speak to the issues, policies, and even the candidates of their day. Many of these sermons are recorded in a two-volume set titled *Political Sermons of the American Founding Era, 1730–1805.*[1]

These pastors wanted their people to be biblically literate so that they could make intelligent decisions about political candidates and social issues based on how they aligned—or didn't align—with the Bible, which is the source of all truth.

Today, we are called to view everything in our world through the lens of the Bible. God's Word is the standard by which we must evaluate all things, and that includes matters in the political realm. It includes identifying the problems we see in the culture around us and offering the solutions to those problems. Through our votes, we can be an influence for righteousness—we can let God's voice be heard in today's culture.

SHOULDN'T THE CHURCH STAY OUT OF POLITICS?

You may be asking, "But what about the separation of church and state? Shouldn't the church stay out of politics?"

The phrase "separation of church and state" is not found anywhere in our founding documents. You won't find it in the Declaration of Independence, the Constitution, or the Bill of Rights.

So where did the phrase come from? We hear it used a lot, and the common perception is that it means

Christians shouldn't let their beliefs shape how they vote or engage in politics. But that's not the case at all.

In 1802, President Thomas Jefferson received a request to answer a question about religious freedom from the Danbury Baptists of Connecticut. In his response—which was a personal letter and not a government edict—Jefferson explained that the First Amendment provides "a wall of separation between Church & State,"[2] protecting the church from government intrusion. The First Amendment was written, in part, to keep the government out of the business of the church, not the church out of the business of government.

However, over the years, the phrase "separation of church and state" has been used to remove God from the public square and to keep the church from having any influence upon the government. It has also intimidated many pastors from speaking in the pulpit about matters that are political in nature.

In 1954, Congress took a step toward restricting the speech of nonprofit tax-exempt entities, including churches. Senator Lyndon B. Johnson proposed an amendment to the Internal Revenue Code that said 501(c)(3) organizations could not "participate in, or intervene in (including the publishing or distributing of statements), any political campaign on behalf of (or in opposition to) any candidate for public office."[3]

It's important to point out that the amendment is limited to prohibiting churches and charities from advocating or opposing specific candidates for office. It does *not* restrict all forms of political engagement. For example, it does not forbid receiving election registrations to vote and recruiting election officers. But there are many who incorrectly assume the amendment prohibits churches from engaging in any political activity at all, under the threat of losing their tax-exempt status.

At the time of this writing, the Johnson Amendment is currently being challenged in the US District Court for the Eastern District of Texas because it prohibits free speech.[4] The Alliance Defending Freedom—a Christian law firm with a significant national and US Supreme Court presence—contends likewise, saying, "Pastors have a right to speak about Biblical truths from the pulpit without fear of punishment. No one should be able to use the government to intimidate pastors into giving up their constitutional rights."[5]

While it's nice for churches to benefit from their tax-exempt status, that shouldn't cause pastors to stay silent about what God has instructed them to say. When pastors fail to speak up because they fear losing their church's tax exemption, they are bowing to the government instead of to God.

As we saw earlier, pastors have been faithful about

helping Christians to use God's Word to evaluate the world around them, including all things political. And today, churches should continue to encourage Christians to vote according to their personal consciences and biblical values.

TO VOTE IS BIBLICAL

God has always intended for Christians to have a positive influence on the culture around them. For us to make scripturally informed decisions about whom to vote for and which policies to support is not being political at all, it is being biblical. Here's why: The culture has hijacked the narrative on social and moral issues that God addresses in the Bible, and it has twisted those social and moral issues into political issues. Then it has told pastors like me and Christians like you to stop being political.

God had a say on all of today's issues long before the word *political* existed. In the Bible, God speaks about life, marriage, parental authority, biological sex, national borders, immigration, economic prosperity, Israel, and even the environment. God had the first word on all these matters and more. And it's important for us to understand that much of what are now called political issues have always been biblical issues.

As Christians, we're to look at what is happening in our culture—including during election season—and we're to view candidates and policies in the light of what

Scripture teaches. That doesn't mean we should expect candidates and their policies to align perfectly with the Bible—that's an unrealistic expectation I'll address more in a moment. But if we want to bring positive change to America, a crucial way to do that is by voting.

If Christians would come together and vote their values, we can help bring positive change to America. There are some people who say that Christians who let the Bible inform their voting decisions are Christian nationalists. But that's a contrived label used to intimidate believers who love God and their country and discourage them from advocating for biblical values in the political process. It's a disparaging term that the political left uses to accuse the church of trying to turn America into a theocracy. The truth is that there will never be a theocracy until Jesus returns.

As Christians, we should desire to have a positive influence on America. We understand the importance of religious freedom, and we recognize that the values taught in the Bible are good for society. As Psalm 33:12 says, "Blessed is the nation whose God is the LORD."

STAYING ALERT TO DANGER

More than ever today, the freedoms that we enjoy and the country we love are in jeopardy. And God calls His people to be watchmen, as we see in Ezekiel 33:1-5:

Again the word of the LORD came to me, saying, "Son of man, speak to the children of your people, and say to them: 'When I bring the sword upon a land, and the people of the land take a man from their territory and make him their watchman, when he sees the sword coming upon the land, if he blows the trumpet and warns the people, then whoever hears the sound of the trumpet and does not take warning, if the sword comes and takes him away, his blood shall be on his own head. He heard the sound of the trumpet, but did not take warning; his blood shall be upon himself. But he who takes warning will save his life.'"

In ancient Israelite cities, a watchman would be assigned to stand guard on the city walls to keep an eye out for approaching enemies or potential attacks. Any time the watchman saw an impending threat, he would blow a trumpet. Then it was up to the people to heed the sound of the warning and save their lives. If they didn't, then their lives might very well be required of them, and the watchman would not be responsible because he had done his job.

Likewise, we as Christians should keep a watch on what is happening around us. And when we see our freedoms and country in danger, we ought to sound the trumpet. I say that not as hyperbole but because of the downward slide we've seen in our country and culture over the past few decades.

We should be proud to be Americans because of what Americans have accomplished for the good of the world, and we should be grateful because of the benefits we enjoy as citizens of this country. But we should also be concerned for our country's future. However, that doesn't mean we should look to a political figure to save our nation from its precipitous descent. Our faith should never be placed in a human leader. Rather, our faith should be placed in the Savior alone—in Jesus, who is the only true hope for America.

But until Jesus comes again, He has charged us with being His ambassadors and representing Him to this world. We are to be like salt and light (Matthew 5:13-14). In Bible times, salt was widely used as a preservative to prevent decay. It works as an antiseptic that has a purifying effect, which is what we're to do as Christians. We're also to shine the light of truth into a dark world.

Political engagement is one very significant way we can be ambassadors as well as salt and light. And by political engagement, I mean the following:

- advocating for policies that promote righteousness

- voting for candidates who most closely represent our biblical values

- praying for our elected leaders and holding them accountable

- running for elected office

If Christians are not politically engaged, guess what will fill the vacuum? Every evil and demonic practice. We, as the church of Jesus Christ, are God's restraining force against evil. And if the church does not rise up to fight the good fight of faith, who will?

If we abdicate our role and responsibility as ambassadors for Christ and as agents of truth, then evil will triumph. You may have heard the saying, "The only thing necessary for the triumph of evil is for good people to do nothing."[6] So we cannot remain silent. The German theologian Dietrich Bonhoeffer, who stood opposed to Nazi Germany, is reported to have said, "Silence in the face of evil is itself evil and God will not hold us guiltless. Not to speak is to speak. Not to act is to act."

Good government cannot save us, but bad government can destroy us. That's why, when election season approaches, we need to ask this question: What can we do to advance the kingdom of God for the glory of God, and to stem the tide of evil in our land until Jesus comes?

ADVANCING THE KINGDOM OF GOD

All through the Bible, we see God's people affecting public policy and staying politically engaged. The Old Testament prophets—including Moses, Elijah, Daniel, Isaiah, Jeremiah—all spoke truth to power. They all confronted kings. They all influenced national laws and social conscience.

In the New Testament, John the Baptist wasn't afraid to confront King Herod—the most powerful political figure in the region at that time—about his immoral lifestyle.

Even Jesus weighed in on political topics. He didn't disengage Himself. When He was asked about whether it was lawful to pay taxes to Caesar, He said, "Render to Caesar the things that are Caesar's, and to God the things that are God's" (Mark 12:17).

Prior to His crucifixion, when Jesus stood before Pontius Pilate, the governor of Judea warned Him, "Do You not know that I have power to crucify You, and power to release You?" (John 19:10). Note how Jesus responded: "You could have no power at all against Me unless it had been given you from above" (John 19:10-11). Was Jesus being too political when He said that? Jesus didn't shy away from speaking truth to power.

The disciples were bold as well. Peter and John were severely rebuked by the Jewish religious and political leaders of their day for preaching the gospel. They were told "not to speak at all nor teach in the name of

Jesus" (Acts 4:18). Peter and John responded, "Whether it is right in the sight of God to listen to you more than to God, you judge. For we cannot but speak the things which we have seen and heard" (verses 19-20).

Were Peter and John being too political when they said that? Or were they being biblical?

All through Scripture, we see consistent evidence of God's people integrating their faith with politics. And they were being biblical when they did so.

DOING OUR PART IN GOD'S WORK

With those examples before us, I want to share three principles for how we can advance the kingdom of God for the glory of God, and stem the tide of evil in our land until Jesus comes.

1. Recognize That God Uses Flawed, Sinful People

When it comes to elections, too often Christians decide they won't vote for a candidate because he or she doesn't align with all their expectations. They say, "There are a few things I don't like about either candidate's personality or policies. So I'm going to sit out this election."

Yes, elections are serious business, and yes, they have serious consequences. But consider this: How often are we able to make decisions in our life that are 100 percent to our liking? When we choose a church, we won't get 100 percent of what we would like when it comes to the music, the preaching, the youth ministry, the missions outreach, the women's ministry, and a host of other things. A church will be strong in some areas and weak in others. Because no church is perfect, we'll select a church based on getting the majority of what's important to us.

The same is true about marriage. When people choose a spouse, they go with someone who has the most of what they desire in a marriage partner. There is no perfect husband or wife.

This principle applies to every area of life—there is no perfect job, no perfect school, no perfect neighborhood, no perfect family. And in elections, there are no perfect candidates. Jesus is not on the ballot.

When we vote, we must let go of the idea that elections are personality contests. Instead, we should focus on the fact we're voting for policies that will inform the government of how it is to conduct itself and how it is to fulfill its responsibilities to society. We are to choose men and women who best represent a biblical worldview in terms of what policies they will create and support. That's because personalities come and go, but policies will live on long after a leader is gone. A nation can thrive when good policies are in place.

When we vote, instead of looking for an ideal candidate, we should vote for the better choice. We can vote, as much as possible, with Proverbs 14:34 in mind: "Righteousness exalts a nation, but sin is a reproach to any people." Every candidate is a flawed, sinful human being. So let's look carefully at their policies and choose to support those who come closest to representing our biblical worldview and convictions.

The Bible makes it clear that righteous leaders will have times when they fail and make unrighteous choices. King David was an upright leader, a man after God's own heart (1 Samuel 13:14). But he committed adultery (2 Samuel 11:1-4), and in an attempt to take some of the glory that belonged to the Lord, he counted the number of his fighting men, allowing his focus to be on the strength of his army rather than the strength of his God (2 Samuel 24:10-13). In both cases, he incurred God's wrath. Still, God used David.

Hezekiah was a righteous king, but the way he handled his foreign policy brought God's judgment upon the nation (2 Kings 20:12-18). Samson started out as a righteous judge, but he had a weakness for women, among other issues. But in the end, God used Samson for the benefit of Israel, and he was included in the Hebrews 11 hall of faith.

The Bible is equally clear that God can use unrighteous leaders to carry out His righteous purposes. He used pagan rulers like King Nebuchadnezzar of Babylon and King Cyrus of Persia to implement policies that benefited Israel and the Jewish people.

The fact God can use righteous yet flawed leaders as well as unrighteous leaders doesn't mean we should excuse sinful behavior. Every one of these leaders paid consequences for his sin. But we must recognize that God is able to use flawed, sinful people to promote good policies for a nation.

And we can vote for leaders with their policies in mind.

When it comes time to vote, let's set aside the personalities, and look carefully at their policies. Remember what Jesus said in Luke 18:19? "No one is good but One, that is, God."

There is no perfect candidate, but God can still use the righteous and the unrighteous to accomplish His good purposes, no matter how flawed they are.

Now let's look at the second principle:

2. Vote for Policies over Personalities

During election season, as we consider how we ought to vote, here are seven areas of policy that are clearly addressed in Scripture.

Judges

Isaiah 1:26—"I will restore your judges as at the first, and your counselors as at the beginning.

Afterward you shall be called the city of righteousness, the faithful city."

Good judges will bring righteousness to a land by virtue of their decisions. So ask yourself: Which candidate will appoint the best judges and justices? Keep in mind that it is presidents who appoint federal judges and who nominate Supreme Court justices, who can be especially influential.

Border Security

Acts 17:26—"[God] has made from one blood every nation of men to dwell on all the face of the earth, and has determined their preappointed times and the boundaries of their dwellings."

Zechariah 7:10—"Do not oppress the widow or the fatherless, the alien or the poor. Let none of you plan evil in his heart against his brother."

Acts 17:26 informs us that God acknowledges and supports borders. It is He who determines their boundaries. In the time of Joshua, when God divided the land for the 12 tribes of Israel, He gave allotments marked by specific boundaries. This suggests that He is in favor of defending defined borders, which means national defense is important.

At the same time, God's heart is favorable toward the immigrant. Zechariah 7:10 tells us we should not oppress the widow, the fatherless, the poor, nor the alien. By alien, Scripture means immigrants.

But there is a right and legal way for people to enter a country. Christians should be pro-immigration, but in accord with what is rightful and lawful. There are many people who have worked hard, for years, to get legal American citizenship. In contrast, there have been many millions who have entered the country illegally, often at the expense of our national security. When we vote, we need to ask: Who will help provide fair and legal paths to citizenship, and who will best protect our borders and support our national security?

Israel

Genesis 12:3—"I will bless those who bless [Israel], and I will curse him who curses [Israel]; and in you all the families of the earth shall be blessed."

It's not possible for us to support every policy of a foreign nation because no nation is perfect in its ways. And the same is true in reverse—you won't find a country that supports every policy held by the United States.

To show our support for Israel does not mean we have

to be in blind agreement with all that Israel does. But Scripture is clear about the fact God will treat nations based on how they treat Israel. Those who are allies with Israel will be blessed, and those who oppose Israel will be cursed.

When we look at the overall context of God's promise to Abraham in Genesis 12:3, we see that it is an everlasting promise—which means it still applies even today. That's why we cannot have political leaders who cozy up to Israel's enemies.

When we vote, let's remember to ask: Which candidate will best support Israel?

Religious Liberty

Exodus 20:3—"You shall have no other gods before Me."

This is the first of the Ten Commandments, and we can appropriately call it a "conscience clause." This verse is a proof text that our allegiance belongs entirely to God, and we should not be required to bow down or submit to anything or anyone that conflicts or competes with our loyalty to Him.

Here are some ways that Christians exercise this conscience clause with respect to religious liberty:

- doctors who object to performing abortions

- bakers and photographers who decline to provide their services for same-sex wedding ceremonies

- employers who decline to provide abortifacient drugs as part of their healthcare program

- employees who object to being required to take a vaccine

When we vote, we need to ask: Which candidate will best support religious liberty, and not force people to violate their conscience or their allegiance to God?

Biological Sex

Genesis 1:27—"God created man in His own image; in the image of God He created him; male and female He created them."

God assigns biological sex in the womb. People don't get to decide they want to be a different gender. To support or legitimize the changing of a person's gender is to contribute to mental disorder or illness.[7] Rather, we should seek to help an individual to understand and celebrate the beautiful way God designed him or her.

Booker T. Washington is credited with saying, "A lie doesn't become truth, wrong doesn't become right, and evil doesn't become good just because it's accepted by a majority."

Which candidate will best protect God's design of biological sex?

Family

> *Psalm 127:3*—"Behold, children are a heritage from the LORD, the fruit of the womb is a reward."

In recent decades, we have seen parental rights incrementally stripped away. Parents have had to fight when places like public schools and healthcare facilities have refused to inform them about the education and medical treatment their children receive. God designed the family, and He entrusted children to parents. Children don't belong to the state; they belong to God, who designed for parents to care for them. When a government interferes with how parents raise their children, it violates God's design.

Who will best support the family and parents' rights?

Life

> *Acts 3:15*—God is called "the Author of life" (ESV).

> *Proverbs 6:17*—God hates "hands that shed innocent blood."

Tragically, it has become more and more difficult to find truly pro-life candidates running for office. Almost all candidates support abortion to some extent—some up to a certain limit, and others up until birth. Because nearly 95 percent of all abortions are performed within the first 15 weeks, even those who advocate for a 15-week ban are effectively supporting 95 percent of all abortions.[8] And as pro-life activist Seth Gruber says, "Those who murder the unborn cannot be trusted to govern the born."[9]

So the question for us is this: Which candidate will more closely protect life?

Of course, these seven issues are not the only ones to consider, but the application of Scripture to these seven areas of policy should give you a sense for how we can apply God's Word to other issues as well. As I mentioned earlier, many of today's political issues are social and moral issues God has already addressed in the Bible. The more we familiarize ourselves with the teachings of Scripture, the more we will develop the kind of discernment that enables us to vote with a biblical perspective. As we look at the world through the lens of the Bible, we gain much clarity.

This now brings us to our third principle for advancing God's kingdom and stemming the tide of evil. The first two are (1) to recognize that God uses flawed, sinful people, and (2) to vote for policies over personalities. Next, we are to…

3. Understand That Voting Is Not Only a Right, It Is a Duty

In Luke 12, Jesus taught a parable about two servants who worked for the same master. Before departing for a trip, the master entrusted his work and possessions to the servants. Upon returning, the master called on the servants to give an account of their stewardship.

As it turned out, one servant was evil and did not carry out the responsibilities given to him. The other was a wise and faithful servant who was careful with what the master had entrusted to him. Jesus concluded the parable by saying, "For everyone to whom much is given, from him much will be required" (verse 48).

Likewise, God has entrusted us with the wonderful privilege of living in the United States of America. Presently, the Master is gone, but He is coming again, and we must be prepared to give an account of all that He has entrusted to our care. As citizens, we have been given stewardship of the freedoms enjoyed in this country. To us, much has been given. Yet as we all know, our freedoms do not come to us free. They come at a cost and must be maintained.

What are we doing with what God has entrusted to us? Are we going to complain and say, "I don't like this, and I don't like that. So I'm going to sit out this election, and let everybody else vote"?

While we might not always like our choices, when we exclude ourselves from the voting process, we have no one to blame except ourselves when wicked policies prevail. I don't mean for this to sound disparaging, but every election is always about choosing the lesser of two evils.

As those who are ambassadors and salt and light, we are to fulfill our biblical mandate to have a positive influence on the culture around us. Which is why we should see voting as a duty. Because if we do nothing—if we check out or remain silent—evil will rush into the vacuum. That's why it's incumbent upon every one of us to be engaged in politics. While it may be difficult to vote, the alternative is far worse.

It is said that there are 90 million self-identified evangelicals in America who are eligible to vote. But of those 90 million, 40 million do not vote, and 15 million are not even registered to vote.[10] If those estimates are correct, that's 55 million self-identified evangelical Christians who are saying, "I'll let evil take over because I'm going to do nothing."

As we saw earlier, "Righteousness exalts a nation" (Proverbs 14:34). Having a righteous influence on our nation is both a privilege and a duty.

Imagine what would have happened if William Wilberforce had decided not to engage in politics. God used him and his membership in the British parliament to abolish the slave trade in the British colonies. It was his faith that spurred him onward in what turned out to be a 20-year battle to have the Slave Trade Act of 1807 passed. He said, "Let it not be said that I was silent when they needed me."[11]

We should have the same perspective as Frederick Douglass, a former slave who said, "I would unite with anybody to do right and with nobody to do wrong."[12]

In World War II, the United States joined forces with a bad leader, Soviet premier Joseph Stalin, to defeat a worse leader, Adolf Hitler. Sometimes that's what must be done. We find it necessary to say, "I don't like this individual, and I don't agree with all their policies, but I need to help fight a greater evil."

As we look forward to the day when Jesus returns to rule and reign over the earth, may we let God use us, to the best of our ability, to promote righteousness in this land.

WE'RE NOT BEING POLITICAL BUT BIBLICAL

True Christians have never been afraid to address the social evils of their day. The church must be the restraining force against what is wrong in the world around us. So when it comes to engaging in politics, we need to recognize that it's not Christians who are stepping outside God's design for mankind. It is those who snub their noses at God and deviate from His Word who have departed from doing what is right.

There are those who accuse Christians of being political when, in reality, we're being biblical. As a pastor, I haven't left my lane. I've been preaching from the same Bible for the last 30-plus years. I've stood in the same place, preached from the same book, and addressed the same issues all through that time. The sanctity of life from the womb to the tomb? It's in the Bible. The design for marriage to be between one man and one woman? It's in the Bible. God's creation of two biological sexes? It's in the Bible. God's design of multiple races and how all lives matter and are equal before God? It's in the Bible. God's intent for the borders of a nation to be defined and defended? It's in the Bible. God's desire for parents to be responsible caretakers of their children and not the government? It's in the Bible.

These are all biblical issues. Those of us who adhere to Scripture have not left our lane. Rather, those who hold to opposing views and values have jumped the grassy median strip. They've come into our lane, and they are trying to hijack the narrative on social and moral issues—as if a godless generation can tell us what is right and what is wrong.

The more progressive and godless our culture becomes, the more its agenda puts distance between themselves and the church. And the more that culture pushes social and moral issues further left, the more that people like you and me will look extreme—when the reality is we've been standing still. We've stood in the same place all this time. And yet we're labeled as political Christian nationalists and accused of being politically extreme.

But we are not political Christian nationalists. We are practical Christian biblicists who believe that Jesus and His righteous ways are the only hope for America. The only way we can have the kind of influence God intends for us to have is when pastors are teaching the truth, Christians are living the truth, and the world is hearing and seeing the truth through our lives.

That's why it is so essential for us to be engaged politically. Martin Luther is credited with saying, "If you preach the gospel in all aspects with the exception of the issues which deal specifically with your time, you are not preaching the gospel at all."

There's a reason our influence is so important. The government is not the answer for the soul of a nation. Jesus alone is the answer for the soul of America.

WILL WE CONFORM OR TRANSFORM?

From about the fourteenth century BC until about the seventh century BC, the dominant empire in the world was the Assyrian Empire. The Assyrians were a brutal and ruthless people. Whenever they took a city captive, they would rape the women, enslave the children, and filet the men. History teaches us that the Assyrians would often skin people alive and use the skin to adorn walls. Their modus operandi was domination by intimidation.

Around the seventh century BC, the Assyrian Empire started to wane, and the Babylonian Empire ascended to greatness. The Babylonians had a very different way of subjugating people. When the Babylonian army overran Judah and took the Jewish people captive over the course of three successive campaigns and deportations—with the final one taking place in 586 BC with the destruction of Jerusalem—they did not resort to domination by intimidation. Rather, they practiced domination by assimilation.

King Nebuchadnezzar had his army bring thousands of Jewish people to Babylon, a very beautiful, opulent, elegant city. The ancient historian Herodotus wrote about how spectacular Babylon was, and how the Euphrates River glistened in the sunlight as it wove its way through the capital of the empire.

The hanging gardens of Babylon are famously known as one of the seven wonders of the ancient world. With all this splendor, you can imagine what it might have been like for the Jewish prisoners of war to arrive. They stepped into a truly enchanted place, and they had to have been overwhelmed by the city's beauty.

The Hebrew people were then systematically indoctrinated by their Babylonian overlords. They were introduced to a new language, new religion, new culture, new food. They were also given new names. The Babylonians would say, "You are no longer who you were at the time you were taken captive. You now belong to us. You're to become like us."

Many of the Jewish captives ended up being seduced by all that Babylon had to offer. That's the reason so many of them, when they had the opportunity, never returned to Jerusalem. They loved Babylon and became too comfortable. They had become part of the culture.

But there were a few exceptions, and one of them was a teenage Jewish boy by the name of Daniel. He was not impressed by Babylon nor seduced by it. He would never bow down to the culture nor to any of the indoctrination he was exposed to. He knew who he was, he understood who God was, and he was forever faithful to the Lord his God, never forsaking Him.

This made it possible for God to use Daniel to speak truth to power. Daniel would go on to influence three different kings over the course of his life—and he never wavered in his devotion to the Lord God Almighty.

Friend, listen to me on this: Babylon has come to us. We are now in Babylon. There's a new speech, a new culture, a new everything. There are new philosophies.

There's even a new name for you if you don't like your own pronouns or your own names. Babylon is here, and the question for us is this: Will we be conformed to Babylon? Or will we transform Babylon? Because only one or the other is possible.

We will either be squeezed into the mold of today's culture and conform and become like Babylon, or we will do our part to transform Babylon as long as God has given us breath to be His influence in a fallen world, and that's what God calls us to be.

I, for one, want to make a difference. I love our country. I love Jesus supremely, and I know that He is our only hope for this nation. To those pastors and Christians who say, "We shouldn't get involved in hot topics or get political," I believe we can respond, "Then you're not living up to your calling."

Listen: This is the time for Daniels. This is the time for us to follow the examples of the Old Testament prophets, John the Baptist, Jesus, the disciples, and so many others all through the Bible. This is the time for every Christ-follower to engage the culture and be an instrument of change through the person and power of Jesus Christ.

Jesus said to us,

You are the salt of the earth...You are the light of the world. A town built on a hill cannot be hidden. Neither do people light a lamp and put it under a bowl. Instead they put it on its stand, and it gives light to everyone in the house. In the same way, let your light shine before others, that they may see your good deeds and glorify your Father in heaven (Matthew 5:13-16 NIV).

This is our mandate. This is our calling. We must not check out. We must not resign.

Jesus is coming again. And until He comes, He says, "Occupy till I come" (Luke 19:13 KJV).

We are to occupy till He comes.

Until Jesus returns, get out there and vote. Be His ambassadors. Be salt and light. And advance God's kingdom for God's glory and help to stem the tide of evil in our land.

Let your voice be heard. Let your vote be counted. And may God again bring revival to the United States of America.

ENDNOTES

1. Ellis Sandoz, ed., *Political Sermons of the American Founding Era, 1730–1805* (Liberty Fund, 1998).

2. "Jefferson's Letter to the Danbury Baptists," January 1, 1802, *Library of Congress*, https://www.loc.gov/loc/lcib/9806/danpre.html.

3. While the Johnson Amendment was originally passed in 1954, the phrase "(or in opposition to)" was added by Congress in 1987.

4. "Complaint filed over Johnson Amendment's application," *Baptist Press*, August 30, 2024, https://www.baptiststandard.com/news/nation/complaint-filed-over-johnson-amendments-application/.

5. Alliance Defending Freedom Senior Legal Counsel Erik Stanley in "Pulpit Freedom Sunday," *Alliance Defending Freedom*, September 26, 2008, https://adflegal.org/press-release/pulpit-freedom-sunday.

6. This quote is widely attributed to Edmund Burke, an eighteenth-century British statesman and philosopher. But the actual origin of the quote is uncertain.

7. It wasn't until 2013 that The Diagnostic and Statistical Manual of Mental Disorders stated, for the first time, that "gender non-conformity is not in itself a mental disorder." Up until that time, if a person identified as a gender that did not align with their biological sex, they were diagnosed as having Gender Identity *Disorder* (emphasis added). See *Diagnostic and Statistical Manual of Mental Disorders: DSM-5* (Washington, DC: American Psychiatric Association, 2013).

8. Kevin Drum, "Raw Data: Abortions By Week of Pregnancy," *Mother Jones*, April 29, 2019, https://www.motherjones.com/kevin-drum/2019/04/raw-data-abortions-by-week-of-pregnancy/.

9. "Awakening the Church to the Horrors of Abortion: Seth Gruber's 1916 Project," *American Faith*, August 14, 2024, https://americanfaith.com/awakening-the-church-to-the-horrors-of-abortion-seth-grubers-1916-project/.

10. "15M Christians Aren't Registered to Vote: Churches Across US Participating in 'Voter Registration Sunday,'" *CBN*, September 20, 2019, https://www2.cbn.com/news/politics/15m-christians-arent-registered-vote-churches-across-us-participating-voter.

11. This quote widely attributed to William Wilberforce, but when he stated it is unknown and hasn't been ascertained.

12. Frederick Douglass, "The Anti-Slavery Movement," Rochester, New York, 1855. See also P. Foner and Y. Taylor, eds., *Frederick Douglass: Selected Speeches and Writings* (Chicago, IL: Lawrence Hill, 1999), 326.